The History of Printing

James Chenery

Series Editor **Rob Waring**

Level 2 - ⊙

The History of Printing

James Chenery

© 2017 Seed Learning, Inc.

Series Editor: Rob Waring
Acquisitions Editor: Liana Robinson
Copy Editor: Casey Malarcher
Cover/Interior Design: Andy Roh

ISBN: 978-1-9464-5223-8

10 9 8 7 6 5 4 3 2 1
21 20 19 18 17

Contents

Before Books

Before there were books, we told stories. Stories were the way we passed on knowledge to our children and their children. Storytellers were an important part of life. We still do this today.

Learning from each other

Older people shared information through stories and acting. They talked about plants, hunting, weather, seasons, history, and many other things.

Telling stories

Talking about hunting

4

Knowledge to be passed on

At some point, we realized we needed to record our stories and knowledge. People have great memories, but sometimes there is too much to remember.

Things for sale in Kenya

People needed a way to record their sales.

People needed a way to record things. They needed to write things down. It's impossible to remember everything!

Early Writing Systems

At first, we drew pictures or used our handprints to record information.

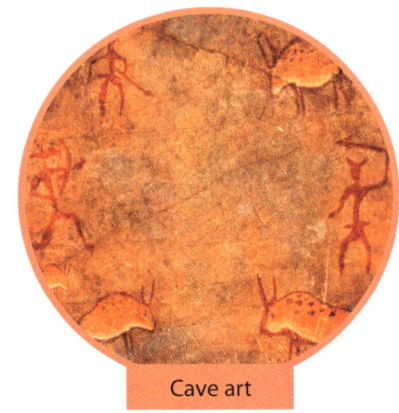
Cave art

But people could not share this knowledge widely as the information was only in one place. People needed a way to make copies of things and share them.

Handprints

A story on the wall of a cave in Algeria

The First Stamps

A name stamp from China, about 1600 BC

The oldest way was to use stamps. People cut marks and lines on soft materials in the shapes they wanted. Then they put it in a liquid and pressed it on things.

The stamps were used for art, to write messages, and to put names on things. These stamps could put patterns on clothes and print pictures and designs.

Indian stamp designs

Wooden stamps for clothes, about 220 BC

7

Ink and Wood Blocks

Wooden print blocks

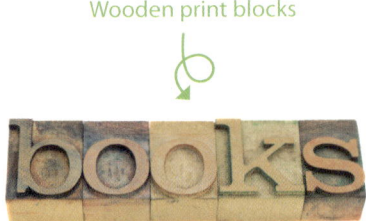

Some people made a few really big stamps to print books. They were called "block books."

Later, the Chinese made many small wooden blocks to print Chinese writing. By using one block for each character, they could use the same blocks again and again.

In 1234, the Koreans began to make many small metal blocks for printing. This was the beginning of modern printing.

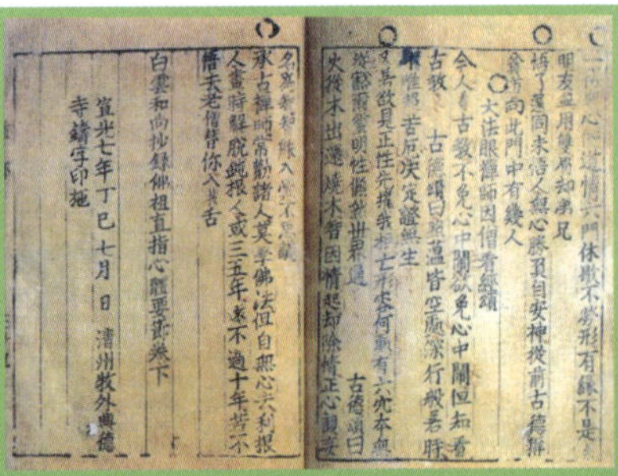

One of the first Korean books printed with movable metal blocks

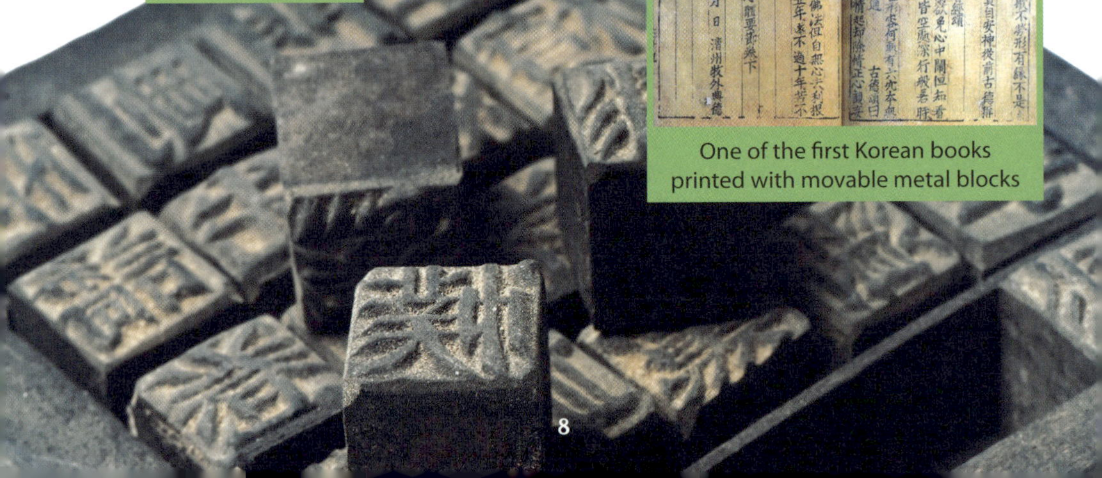

Chinese wooden print blocks

The First Printing Press

Movable metal blocks led to the idea of the first printing machine. It was made by Johannes Gutenberg in Germany about 1450.

Johannes Gutenberg

Gutenberg's press

The printing machine was very large with metal blocks for letters. It was called a "press" because it pushed the paper very hard onto the letter blocks.

It made a very good print and was much faster than writing or printing by hand.

Printing pages

The Printer's Job

To use the machine:

- Arrange the metal letter blocks into words and sentences.
- Put ink on the blocks.
- Put a piece of paper on top of the blocks.
- Use the machine to press the paper against the blocks.

Putting the paper on the machine

Putting on ink

Arranging the letter blocks

The Power of Steam

In 1814, another German named Friedrich Koenig began selling steam-powered printing presses. The steam power was the same idea that was used in trains. But instead of turning train wheels, the steam power turned the wheels of the printing press.

The first steam press

A page from *The London Times*, about 1862

Koenig's first customer was the *London Times* newspaper,

Koenig's steam press

which bought two of his machines. With steam power, the printing press could work much faster than before, allowing them to print hundreds or thousands of copies in a few minutes.

Giant Newspaper Machines

Next came rolling printing presses which put the type onto a cylinder instead of a flat block. That way, the paper could roll through the machine as it was printing.

Preparing the paper

Over time, newspapers began building bigger and bigger presses. They were huge! Some presses could also cut the paper to make the newspapers.

Printing a newspaper

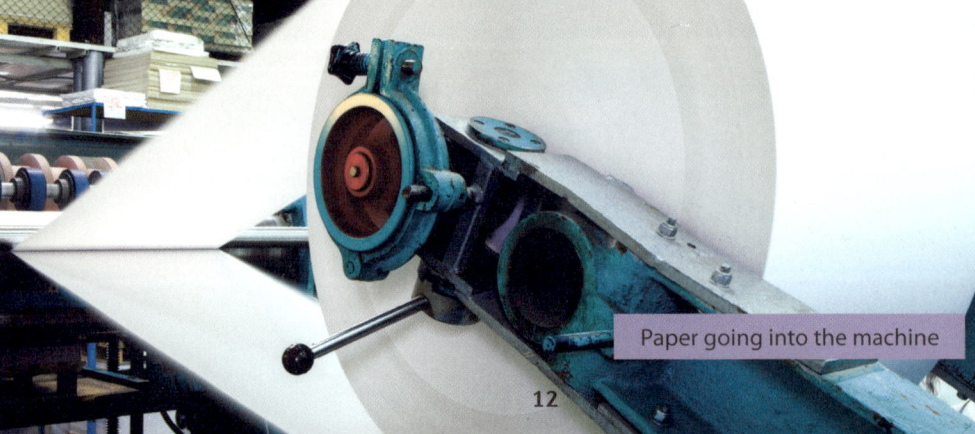
Paper going into the machine

Personal Printing

In the early 20th century, the mimeograph allowed people to print many copies by using a small machine for the office.

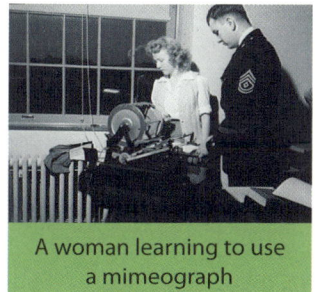

A woman learning to use a mimeograph

Before 1940, the first photocopier was developed. These machines were faster than mimeographs and used dry ink.

Modern photocopiers are very fast and print very well.

Mimeograph

A modern photocopier

Digital Printing

The first computer printers were made in 1968. They were called "dot matrix" because they made letters and pictures from many dots. They were very noisy!

A typical printer today

Computer printers have gotten better and better over the years. Today, most people have a laser printer at home which can print beautiful full-color pictures.

Some bookstores now even have "on-demand" printers. These machines can make a book in minutes—any book in any language!

Dot matrix print

A dot matrix printer

3D Printing Today

3D printers are machines that print objects. Instead of ink, they can print with plastic, metal, glass—even chocolate!

Now, we can print bones to put in our bodies.

The printing process is slow, but anyone can use it to create exciting objects. If you want to, you can change the design every time you print.

3D printers are now making car parts, building materials, food—even bones and body parts.

3D printing in the office

3D printer at work

Space Travel and the Future

The International Space Station is also using 3D printing technology. Scientists use it for research and to make things they need.

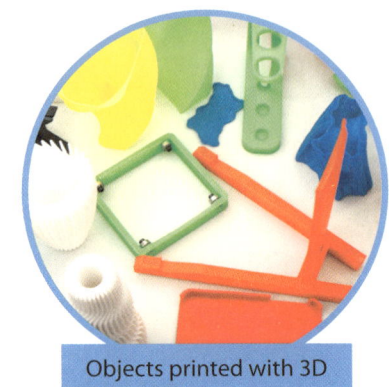

Objects printed with 3D technology

If we can print tools and objects in space, then we can go far from Earth. Someday, we may use 3D printing to make a base on the moon or Mars!

The International Space Station

Looking Back, Looking Ahead

W e have come a long way in our adventures with printing—from leaving our hand prints on cave walls to printing with blocks and stamps. The printing press allowed us to mass-produce books, and the advances in technology in the past 200 years have allowed us to print our own materials at home.

What will we print next?

Now we can print 3D objects, too. In the future, we may be able to print whole space stations.

Who knows what we'll be able to print next?

Will we print a moon base?

An astronaut holding a 3D printed tool

Comprehension Questions

1. How did ancient people remember their culture?
   (a) By telling stories
   (b) By writing books
   (c) By using computers
   (d) All of these

2. What was a problem with handprints and cave drawings?
   (a) They were dirty.
   (b) They were slow.
   (c) They would wash away in the rain.
   (d) They were only in one place.

3. What was the first way to print books?
   (a) With a printer
   (b) With "block book" stamps
   (c) With metal block type
   (d) With steam power

4. What was NOT part of the printer's job?
   (a) To arrange the words
   (b) To put the ink on the blocks
   (c) To press the paper onto the blocks
   (d) To make the ink

5. Who invented the steam press?
   (a) The *London Times*
   (b) Johannes Gutenberg
   (c) Friedrich Koenig
   (d) The Chinese

6. What do most people have at home these days?
   (a) A dot matrix printer
   (b) An "on-demand" printer
   (c) A printing press
   (d) A laser printer

7. The first small printer that printed many copies was called a...
   (a) printing press.
   (b) photocopier.
   (c) dot matrix printer.
   (d) mimeograph.

8. Which technology came first?
   (a) Dot matrix
   (b) Laser
   (c) "On-demand" printing
   (d) Photocopier

9. 3D printing is different because it...
   (a) is fast.
   (b) can print objects.
   (c) can print on paper.
   (d) prints small dots.

10. In the future, we might be able to print...
    (a) digital books.
    (b) space stations.
    (c) people.
    (d) stamps.

Key 1. (a) 2. (d) 3. (b) 4. (d) 5. (c) 6. (d) 7. (d) 8. (d) 9. (b) 10. (b)

Glossary

- **base** the main place where a person lives or works

- **cave** a large hole in the side of a mountain

- **cylinder** a shape with circular ends and long, straight sides

- **dot matrix printer** a computer printer that forms letters, numbers, and symbols from small dots

- **laser** a high power light that can be used for printing

- **liquid** a substance, like water, that is not solid and you can pour easily

- **mass-produce** to make a lot of goods cheaply using machines in a factory

- **mimeograph** an early personal printing machine

- **movable** able to put in another place or position

- **on-demand** available when needed or wanted

- **pattern** a design of lines, shapes, colors, etc.

- **photocopier** a machine that makes copies of papers with writing on them by photographing them

- **stamp** a tool, often a carved block, for putting a special ink mark on something

- **steam** the gas that comes from heating water

Image Credit/Pages

World History Timeline

This chart shows a rough overview of world history.
Some of the dates have been simplified.

World History Timeline

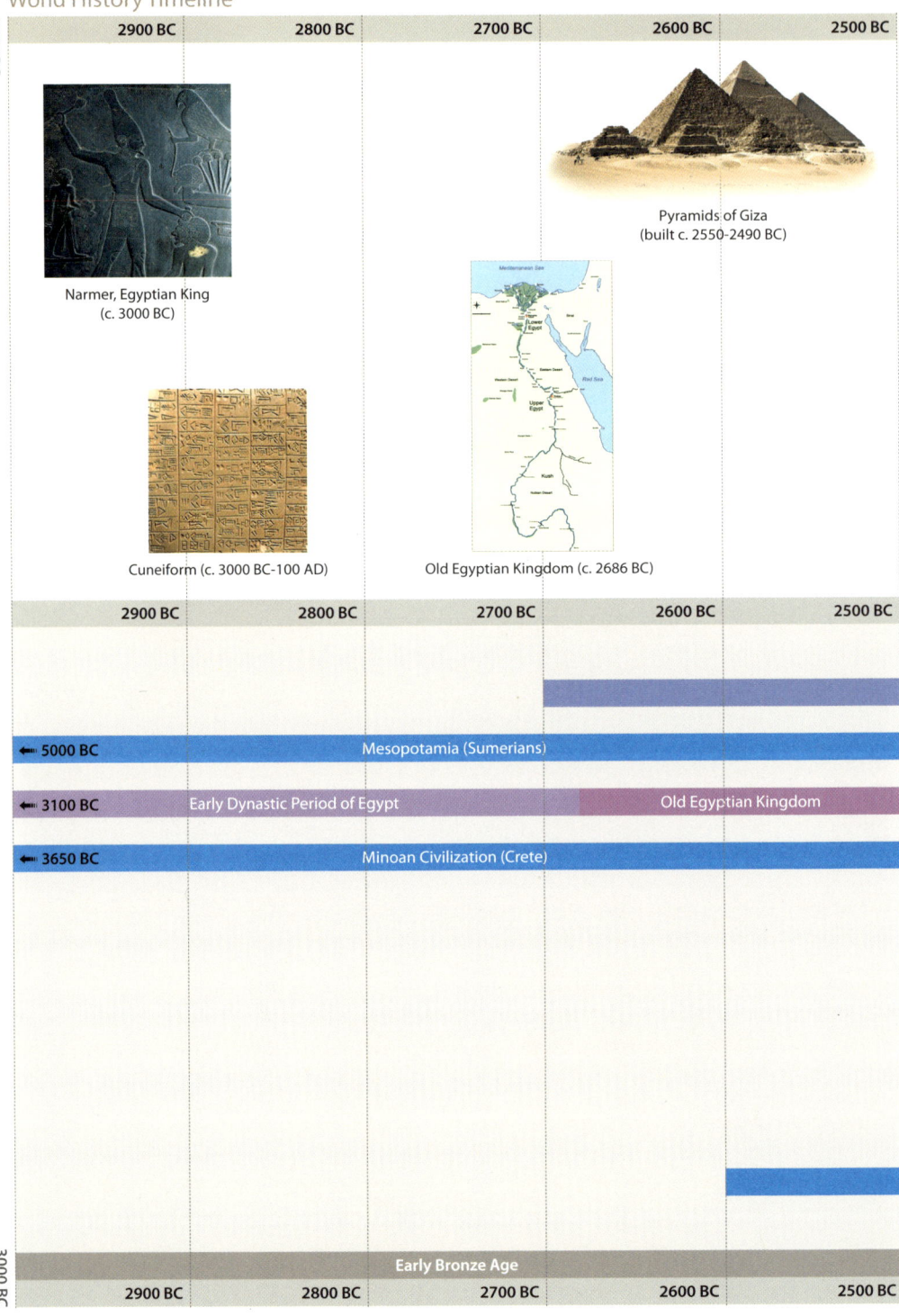

3000 BC	2900 BC	2800 BC	2700 BC	2600 BC	2500 BC

Narmer, Egyptian King
(c. 3000 BC)

Pyramids of Giza
(built c. 2550-2490 BC)

Cuneiform (c. 3000 BC-100 AD)

Old Egyptian Kingdom (c. 2686 BC)

2900 BC	2800 BC	2700 BC	2600 BC	2500 BC

◄ 5000 BC Mesopotamia (Sumerians)

◄ 3100 BC Early Dynastic Period of Egypt Old Egyptian Kingdom

◄ 3650 BC Minoan Civilization (Crete)

Early Bronze Age

2900 BC	2800 BC	2700 BC	2600 BC	2500 BC

3000 BC

2400 BC	2300 BC	2200 BC	2100 BC	2000 BC

Sahure, Egyptian King
(c. 2487-2475 BC)

Indus Valley
Civilization

Sargon the Great,
Akkadian King
(c. 2340-2284 BC)

Gudea of Lagash
(c. 2144-2124 BC)

Ur III Dynasty (c. 2112-2004 BC)

2400 BC	2300 BC	2200 BC	2100 BC	2000 BC

Xia Dynasty

Gutian Dynasty

Elam (Iran)

Akkadian Empire

Ur III Dynasty

Assyria (Early Period)

Middle Egyptian Kingdom

Minoan Civilization (Crete)

1st Intermediate
Period

Indus Valley Civilization (India)

2400 BC	2300 BC	2200 BC	2100 BC	2000 BC

World History Timeline

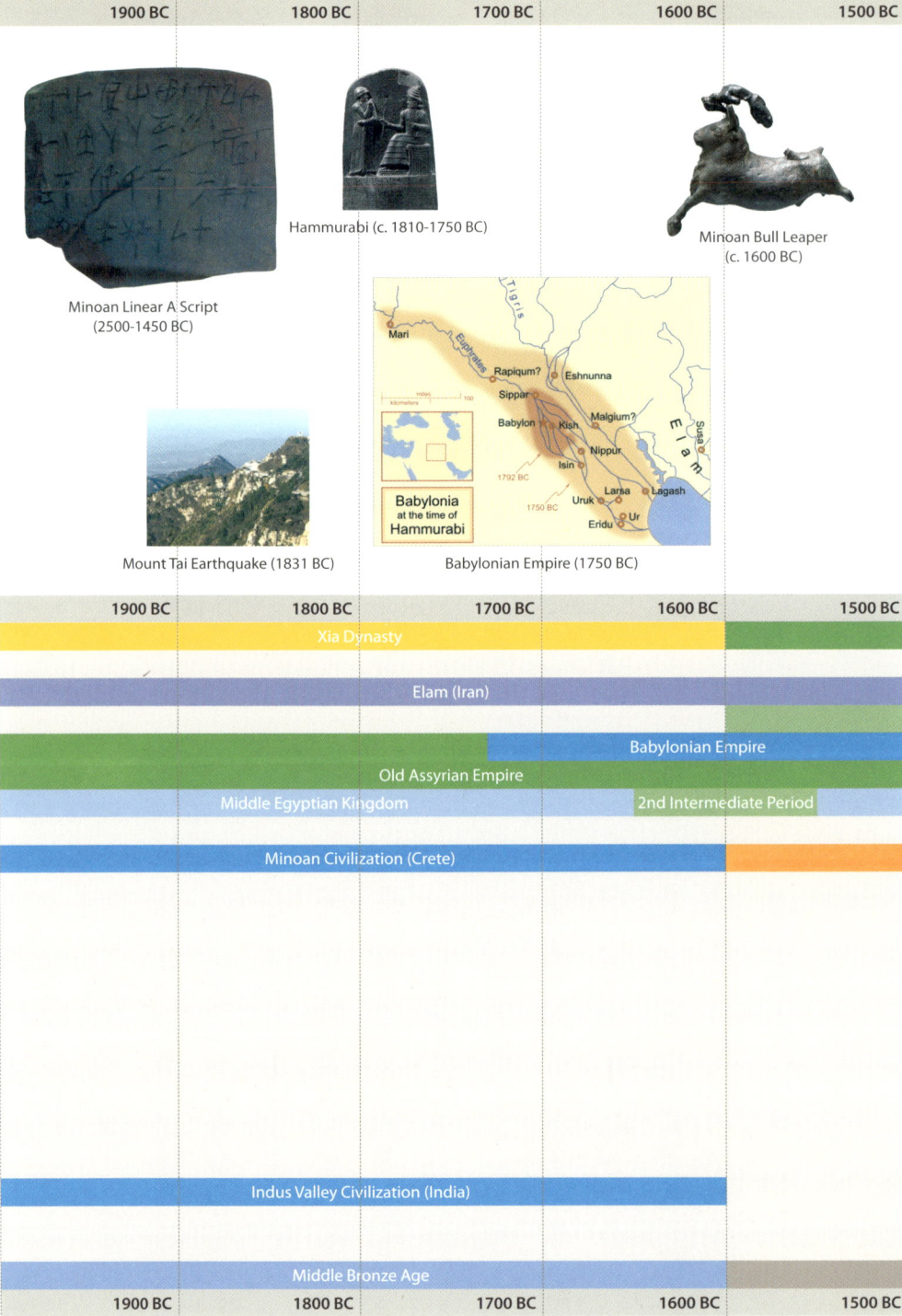

1900 BC	1800 BC	1700 BC	1600 BC	1500 BC

Minoan Linear A Script
(2500-1450 BC)

Hammurabi (c. 1810-1750 BC)

Minoan Bull Leaper
(c. 1600 BC)

Mount Tai Earthquake (1831 BC)

Babylonia
at the time of
Hammurabi

Babylonian Empire (1750 BC)

1900 BC	1800 BC	1700 BC	1600 BC	1500 BC

Xia Dynasty

Elam (Iran)

Babylonian Empire

Old Assyrian Empire

Middle Egyptian Kingdom

2nd Intermediate Period

Minoan Civilization (Crete)

Indus Valley Civilization (India)

Middle Bronze Age

1900 BC	1800 BC	1700 BC	1600 BC	1500 BC

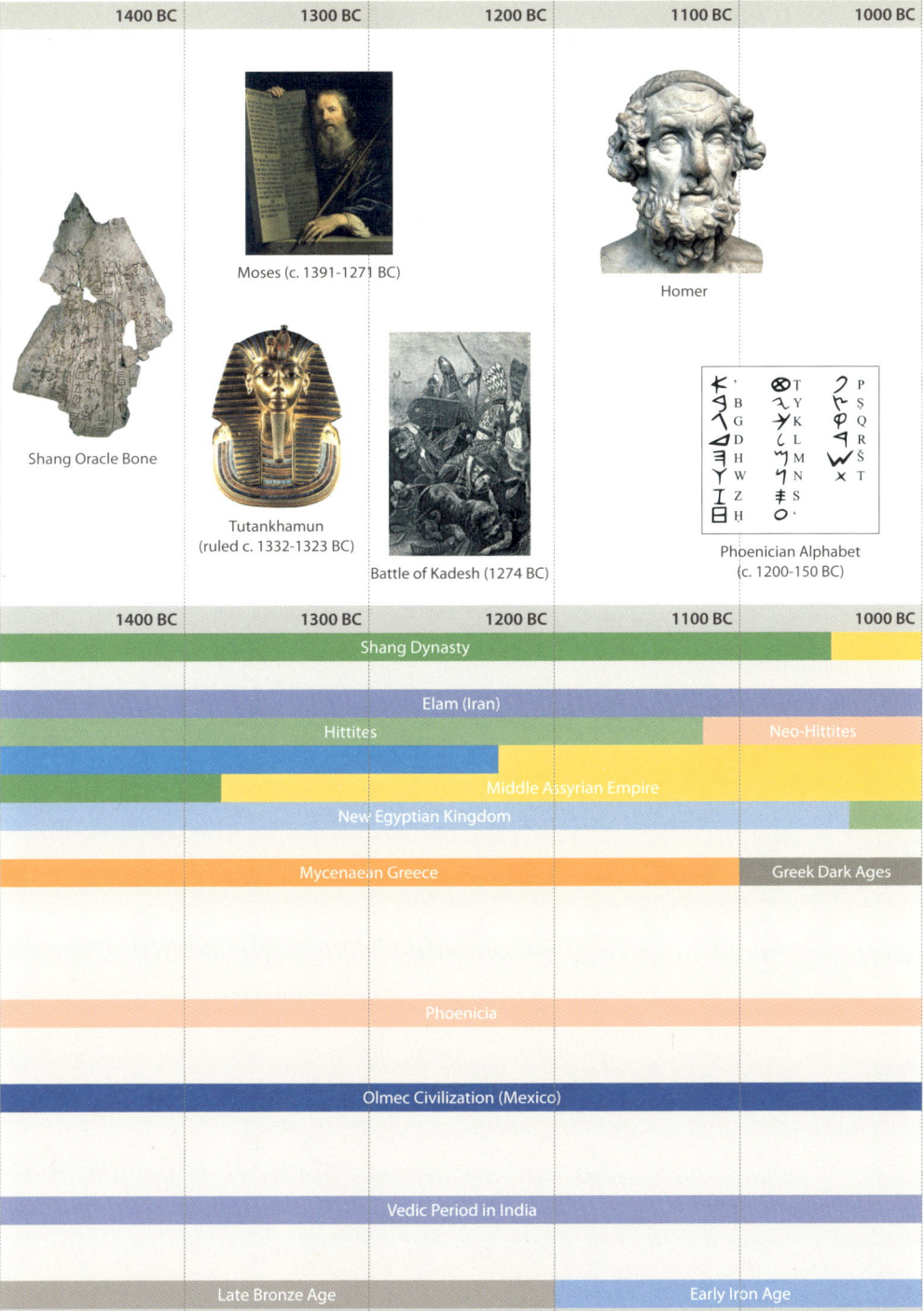

| 1400 BC | 1300 BC | 1200 BC | 1100 BC | 1000 BC |

Moses (c. 1391-1271 BC)

Homer

Shang Oracle Bone

Tutankhamun
(ruled c. 1332-1323 BC)

Battle of Kadesh (1274 BC)

Phoenician Alphabet
(c. 1200-150 BC)

| 1400 BC | 1300 BC | 1200 BC | 1100 BC | 1000 BC |

Shang Dynasty

Elam (Iran)

Hittites

Neo-Hittites

Middle Assyrian Empire

New Egyptian Kingdom

Mycenaean Greece

Greek Dark Ages

Phoenicia

Olmec Civilization (Mexico)

Vedic Period in India

Late Bronze Age

Early Iron Age

| 1400 BC | 1300 BC | 1200 BC | 1100 BC | 1000 BC |

World History Timeline

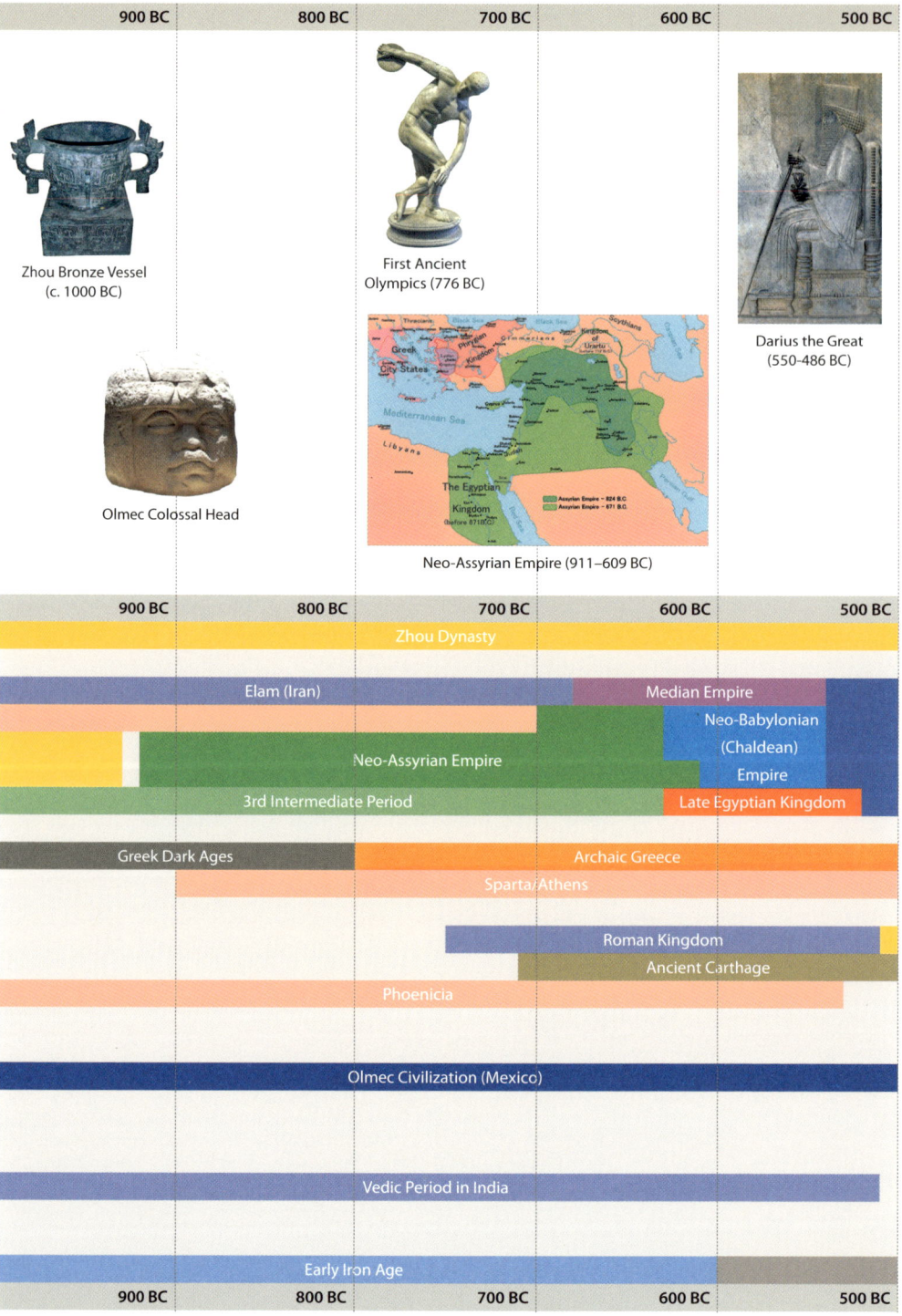

| 900 BC | 800 BC | 700 BC | 600 BC | 500 BC |

Zhou Bronze Vessel (c. 1000 BC)

Olmec Colossal Head

First Ancient Olympics (776 BC)

Neo-Assyrian Empire (911–609 BC)

Darius the Great (550–486 BC)

| 900 BC | 800 BC | 700 BC | 600 BC | 500 BC |

Zhou Dynasty

Elam (Iran)

Median Empire

Neo-Assyrian Empire

Neo-Babylonian (Chaldean) Empire

3rd Intermediate Period

Late Egyptian Kingdom

Greek Dark Ages

Archaic Greece

Sparta/Athens

Roman Kingdom

Ancient Carthage

Phoenicia

Olmec Civilization (Mexico)

Vedic Period in India

Early Iron Age

| 900 BC | 800 BC | 700 BC | 600 BC | 500 BC |

400 BC | 300 BC | 200 BC | 100 BC | 0

Alexander the Great
(356-323 BC)

Hannibal
(247-183 BC)

Julius Caesar
(100-44 BC)

Cleopatra
(69-30 BC)

Battle of Salamis
(480 BC)

Seleucid Empire (312-63 BC)

Rossetta Stone
(created 196 BC)

400 BC | 300 BC | 200 BC | 100 BC | 0

Zhou Dynasty

Qin

Han Dynasty

Achaemenid (Persian) Empire

Alexander the Great

Parthian Empire

Seleucid Empire
Ptolemaic Kingdom
(Hellenistic Greece)

Classical Greece

Sparta/Athens

Roman Empire

Roman Republic

Roman Empire

Maurya Empire

Middle Iron Age

400 BC | 300 BC | 200 BC | 100 BC | 0

World History Timeline

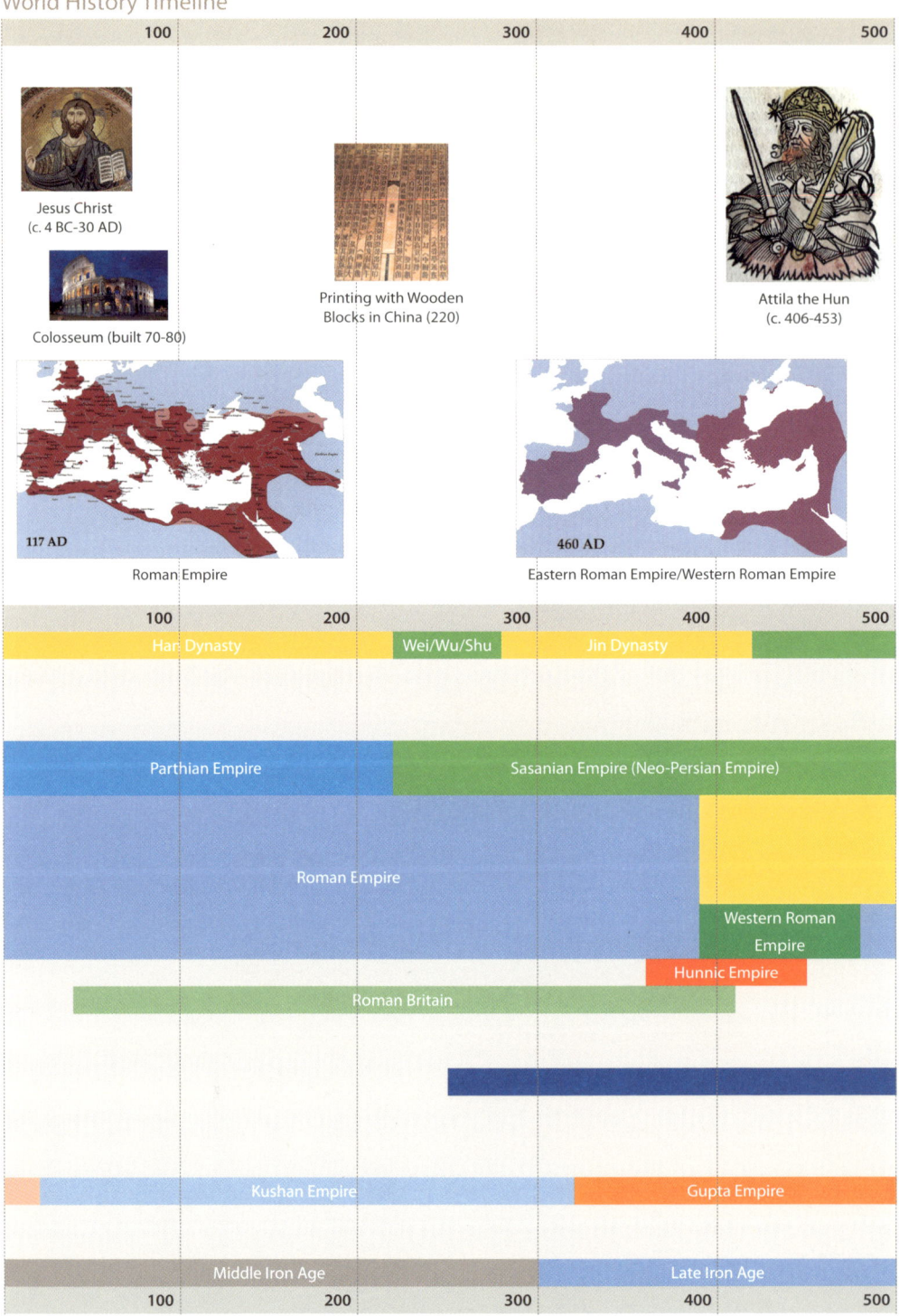

Jesus Christ
(c. 4 BC-30 AD)

Colosseum (built 70-80)

Printing with Wooden
Blocks in China (220)

Attila the Hun
(c. 406-453)

117 AD

Roman Empire

460 AD

Eastern Roman Empire/Western Roman Empire

| | 100 | 200 | 300 | 400 | 500 |

Han Dynasty

Wei/Wu/Shu

Jin Dynasty

Parthian Empire

Sasanian Empire (Neo-Persian Empire)

Roman Empire

Western Roman Empire

Hunnic Empire

Roman Britain

Kushan Empire

Gupta Empire

Middle Iron Age

Late Iron Age

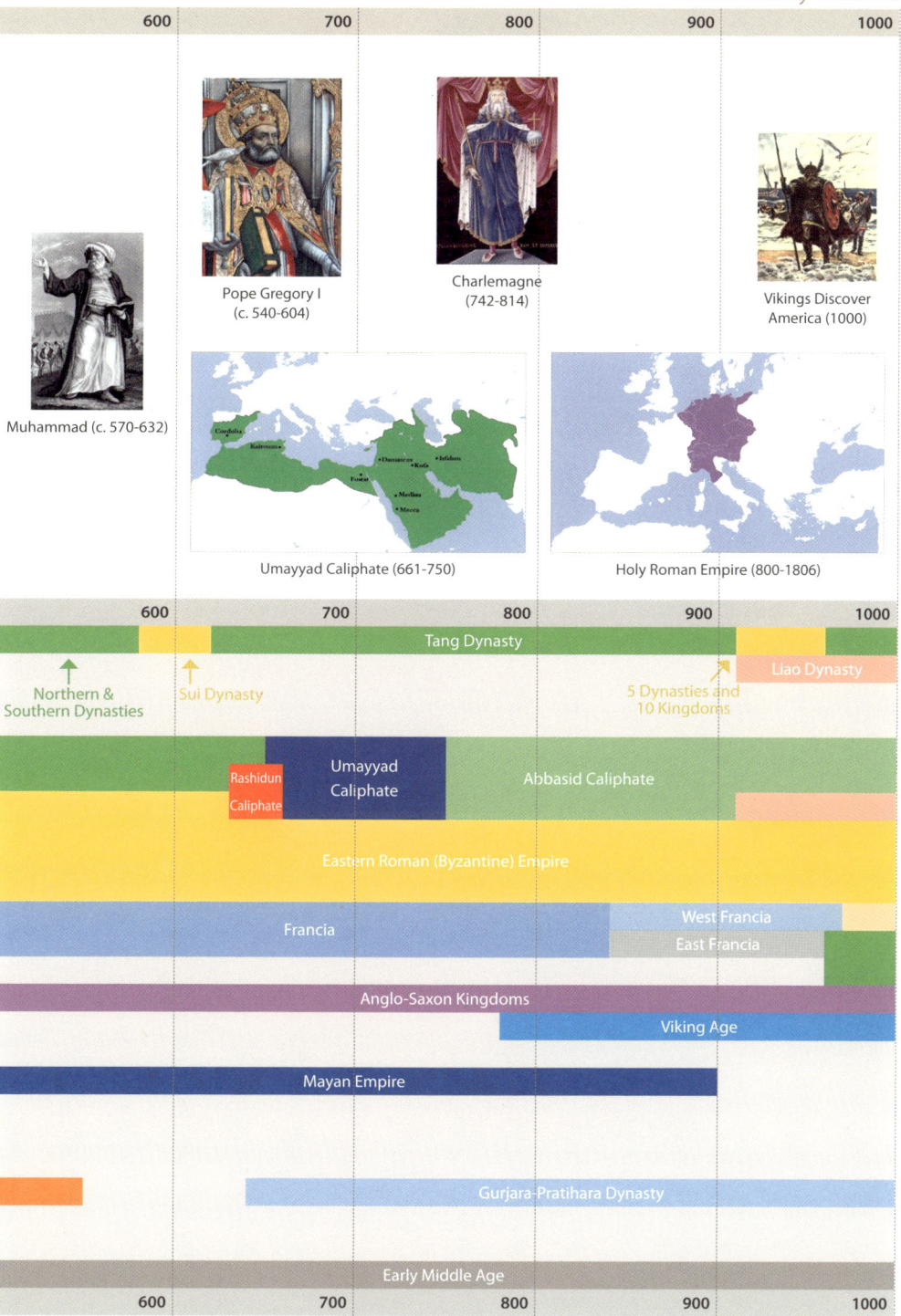

600 · 700 · 800 · 900 · 1000

Pope Gregory I
(c. 540-604)

Charlemagne
(742-814)

Vikings Discover
America (1000)

Muhammad (c. 570-632)

Umayyad Caliphate (661-750)

Holy Roman Empire (800-1806)

600 · 700 · 800 · 900 · 1000

Tang Dynasty

Liao Dynasty

Northern &
Southern Dynasties

Sui Dynasty

5 Dynasties and
10 Kingdoms

Rashidun
Caliphate

Umayyad
Caliphate

Abbasid Caliphate

Eastern Roman (Byzantine) Empire

Francia

West Francia

East Francia

Anglo-Saxon Kingdoms

Viking Age

Mayan Empire

Gurjara-Pratihara Dynasty

Early Middle Age

600 · 700 · 800 · 900 · 1000

World History Timeline

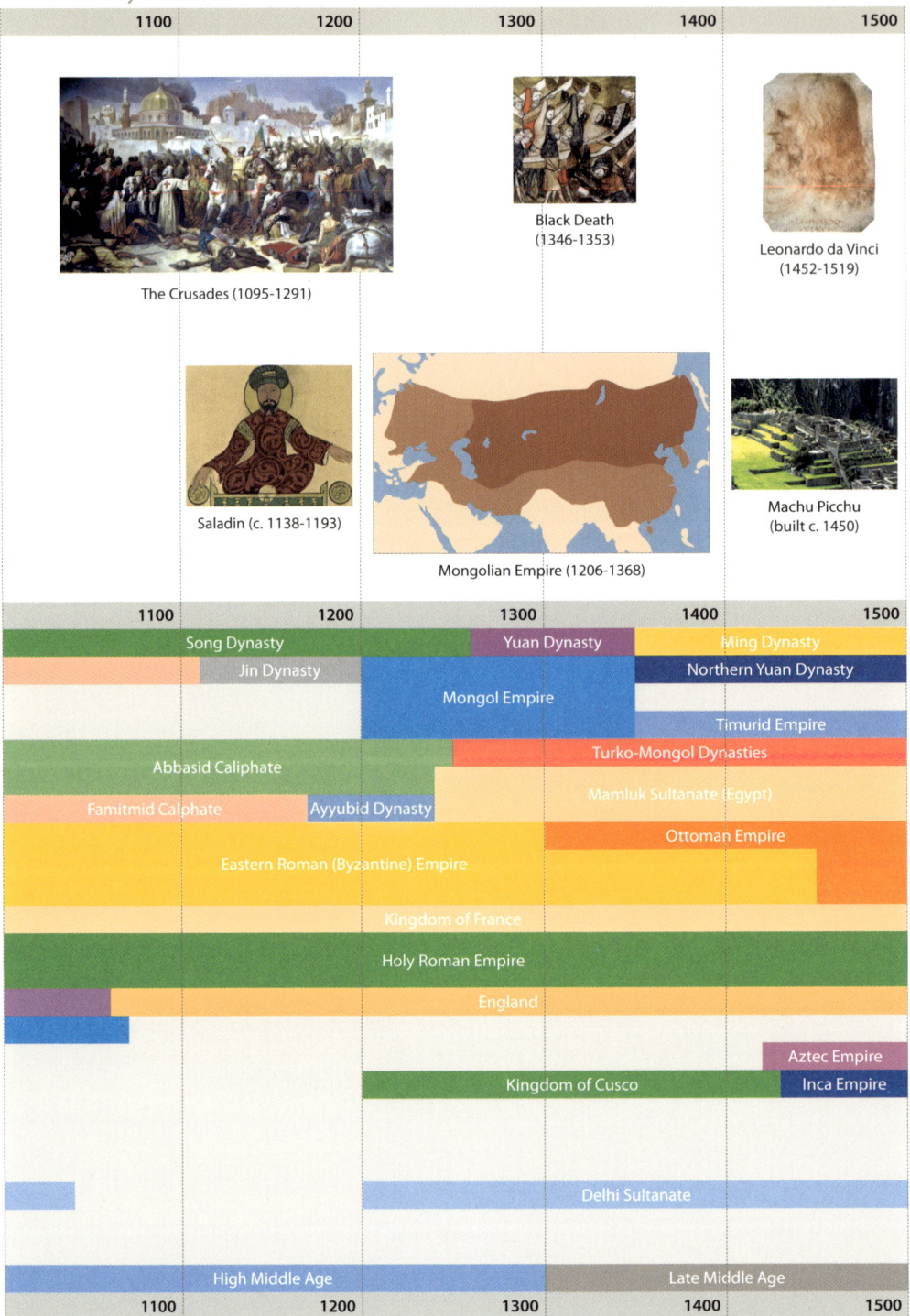

The Crusades (1095-1291)

Black Death (1346-1353)

Leonardo da Vinci (1452-1519)

Saladin (c. 1138-1193)

Mongolian Empire (1206-1368)

Machu Picchu (built c. 1450)

	1100	1200	1300	1400	1500

Song Dynasty

Yuan Dynasty

Ming Dynasty

Jin Dynasty

Northern Yuan Dynasty

Mongol Empire

Timurid Empire

Abbasid Caliphate

Turko-Mongol Dynasties

Famitmid Calphate

Ayyubid Dynasty

Mamluk Sultanate (Egypt)

Eastern Roman (Byzantine) Empire

Ottoman Empire

Kingdom of France

Holy Roman Empire

England

Aztec Empire

Kingdom of Cusco

Inca Empire

Delhi Sultanate

High Middle Age

Late Middle Age

	1100	1200	1300	1400	1500

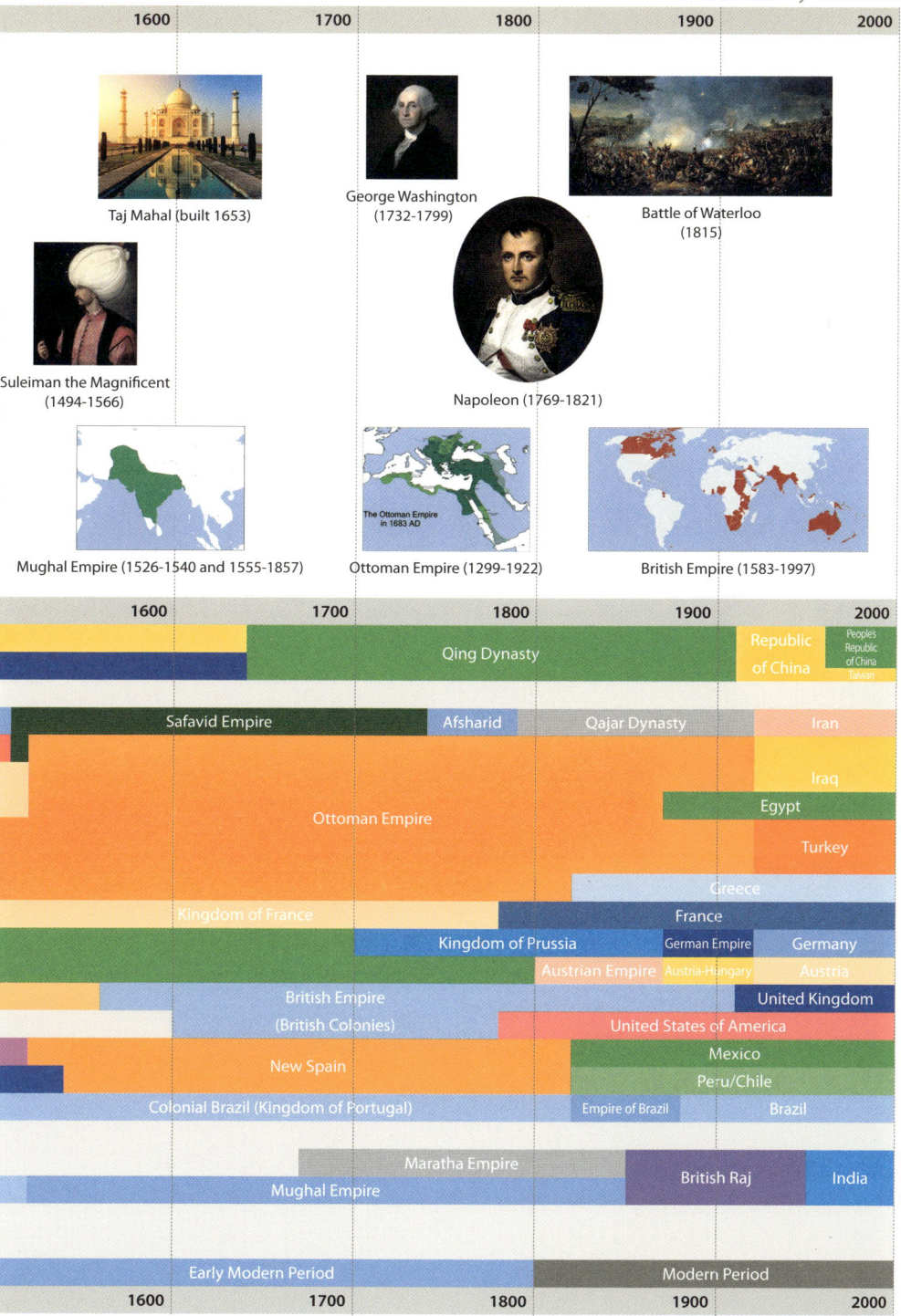

World History Timeline

Taj Mahal (built 1653)

George Washington (1732-1799)

Battle of Waterloo (1815)

Suleiman the Magnificent (1494-1566)

Napoleon (1769-1821)

Mughal Empire (1526-1540 and 1555-1857)

Ottoman Empire (1299-1922)

British Empire (1583-1997)

Qing Dynasty — Republic of China — Peoples Republic of China / Taiwan

Safavid Empire — Afsharid — Qajar Dynasty — Iran

Iraq

Ottoman Empire — Egypt — Turkey

Greece

Kingdom of France — France

Kingdom of Prussia — German Empire — Germany

Austrian Empire — Austria-Hungary — Austria

British Empire — United Kingdom

(British Colonies) — United States of America

New Spain — Mexico

Peru/Chile

Colonial Brazil (Kingdom of Portugal) — Empire of Brazil — Brazil

Maratha Empire — British Raj — India

Mughal Empire

Early Modern Period — Modern Period

List of Books

LEVEL 1

1. Calendars and the History of Time
2. Searching for El Dorado
3. The Tower of Babel
4. The Pilgrim Fathers
5. Traveling on the Silk Road
6. The Invention of Writing
7. The Making of a United Europe
8. The Magic of Numbers
9. The Persian Empire
10. The Great Wall of China

LEVEL 2

1. The Ottomans and Their Empire
2. The War Between the States
3. The Industrial Revolution
4. The Agricultural Revolution
5. Wars in the Middle East
6. The British Empire, Then and Now
7. The Neo-Assyrian Empire
8. The Rise and Fall of Communism
9. The History of Printing
10. The Vikings and Erik the Red

LEVEL 3

1. Space Exploration
2. The Spanish Conquest of the Americas
3. Cleopatra
4. The French Revolution
5. Benjamin Franklin
6. Galileo Galilei
7. The Battle of Salamis
8. Tea and Wars
9. Christopher Columbus
10. The Trojan War

LEVEL 4

1. Alexander the Great
2. Leonardo da Vinci
3. The Neo-Babylonian Empire
4. The Birth of the United States of America
5. Life and Death in Ancient Egypt
6. Life in the Roman Army
7. The Great Plane Race
8. Genghis Khan
9. Korea: A Land Divided by War
10. The Crusades

LEVEL 5

1. The Story of the Renaissance
2. The Great Plague
3. The Mughal Empire
4. Popes and Kings in the Middle Ages
5. Tutankhamun
6. The Story of the Reformation
7. The Medical Revolution
8. Decisive Battles of World War II
9. China: The New Superpower
10. The Great Depression

LEVEL 6

1. World War I
2. Communication Technology
3. The First Democracies
4. The Cold War
5. Global Trade and Peace
6. Greek Culture
7. Napoleon
8. The History of Transportation
9. Capitalism: Good or Evil?
10. China's First Empire: The Qin Dynasty